Abraham Lincoln:

Written by Robert Hogrogian
Illustrated by Pat Tamburri

JANUARY PRODUCTIONS

Library of Congress Catalog Card Number: 79-90162
ISBN: 0-934898-46-4 (library edition)
ISBN: 0-934898-05-7 (paperback)

ABRAHAM LINCOLN

It is true that both father and mother of Abe Lincoln could make some claims of belonging to the high society of their day. Thomas Lincoln, his father, could point with pride to the Lincolns of New England while his mother, Nancy, could say that she belonged to one of the first families of Virginia.

But all that was in the past. To Abe Lincoln it meant nothing. Abe's family was very poor. His family lived in a log cabin in Kentucky. Abe had to sleep in a loft on a pile of corn shucks or dry leaves. He wrapped himself in a bearskin to keep away the chill on those cold winter nights.

Tom Lincoln was like many of the frontier men of his day. Frontier life was rough and everyone worked hard to get along. Tom, like many of the others, was restless — always looking for richer land and an easier life. He could not understand his son's thirst for knowledge. To him any interest in books and reading was a sign of laziness.

Nancy Lincoln, on the other hand, was a sensitive person, kind-hearted and religious. Young Abe loved her with all his heart. She sent him and his sister Sally to school whenever she could.

The schools where frontier children learned to read and write were usually very simple cabins, often with no windows for light. They were called "blab" schools because the children learned by shouting their lessons over and over again until they learned them by heart. Abe learned fast.

When Abe was still a young boy, his father decided to move the family to Pigeon Creek, Indiana. He had heard of the rich land in that new state and thought farming would be better there. Tom built only the roughest kind of shelter that first bitter winter — no more than a shed with a roof and three walls. It was known as a "half-faced camp." In the spring he built a one room cabin. There were no windows, but at least it had a fireplace and a door.

Abe helped his father clear the fields. It was hard work but Abe learned quickly to use an axe; in fact, he became very skilled at it. Pioneer life was not easy, but things were starting to look up. That is, until his mother died. Abe was only nine. His world seemed to be completely shattered. He was heartbroken.

Before long Tom Lincoln had remarried. Abe's new mother was a widow with three children. Her name was Sarah Johnson. Abe took to her from the start. It was she who insisted that Abe should be able to "read, write, and do 'rithmetic." Abe came to respect his stepmother — came to love her — and he carried out her wishes.

The children went to a school nine miles from their cabin whenever they could. Although Abe's days in school were few, Abe's thirst for knowledge and love of reading grew and grew. Abe would walk miles to borrow any book he could, but what was there to read? He had only a handful of books: *Aesop's Fables, Pilgrims' Progress, Robinson Crusoe, Benjamin Franklin's Autobiography* and his favorite, Parson Weem's *Life of George Washington*. He read it so often that he knew it by heart. These books became his university. In them he found not only a sense of style for his writings, but also for his conduct in life.

Abe's interest was not only in books. He loved people and could sing and laugh with the best of them. He became a great storyteller. People would often gather around to hear him tell stories of the things he read in books. They enjoyed listening to him; he knew how to make them laugh.

Abe worked hard all his life. Until he reached the age of 21, all the money he made had to be given to his father. He took on any job he could find. When Abe was only nineteen, a rich farmer by the name of James Gentry hired Abe to make a flatboat and, with Gentry's son Allen, take a cargo to New Orleans where it would be sold.

"Ten dollars!" Abe thought. It was a lot of money to Abe.

But it wasn't just the money that interested him. The trip itself was a call to adventure. To him that crude flatboat became the grandest ship that ever sailed and the Mississippi River seemed like the seven seas rolled up in one. He looked forward to seeing first hand the beautiful and glamorous city of New Orleans.

As it turned out, Abe would never forget that trip — not for the fun and adventure, but for the misery he found there. The beautiful city lost its glamour when he saw Blacks on the auction block. The scene was common enough for New Orleans, but Abe could hardly believe his eyes and ears as he watched and listened to the auctioneer:

"What am I bid for this lady? I admit she's old, but there's still some work left in her."

"How about this young buck? Look at him. He's a mighty strong one!"

"Here's a fine young lass. Good-looking, too. I warn you, she'll fetch a fancy price —"

Abe turned away, his heart saddened by the sight. How could people be so hard and unfeeling? Who gave them the right to sell people as if they were cattle?

Abe learned a lot from his trip to New Orleans. When he returned to Indiana, he had even more stories to tell. He told of the hustle and bustle of city life, of the fancy clothes, of the different languages he heard, of river pirates, and, of course, he also told of the slave markets where people were auctioned off like cattle.

When Abe was 21, he and his family moved to Illinois. Tom Lincoln's new farm was doing well, but Abe, no longer under his father's control, decided that farming wasn't for him.

Abe tried clerking at a general store and got a great reputation for his honesty. The store didn't do well, but at least that gave him time to read. When the store finally failed, Abe worked at a number of different jobs before deciding to buy a store with his friend as a partner. Unfortunately, this store failed, too. His partner was never around and Abe was too kind to turn down anyone in need. Again he was out of a job.

Abe turned his attention to politics. He ran for the State Legislature of Illinois in 1832 and lost, but he was comforted by the fact that his own town of New Salem had voted for him. The next election Abe ran again. This time he won. He borrowed money for a new outfit and headed for the state capital.

When the session of the legislature had ended, Abe returned to New Salem. He had fallen in love with a girl named Ann Rutledge. They had made plans to marry, but it was not to be. Ann, only nineteen years of age, died in 1835. Abe, heartbroken, carried a bunch of flowers to her grave.

For a while, Abe felt lost in grief. In time, however, he managed to pull himself together and carry on. He ran again for the state legislature and was re-elected. Not only that — this young man who never had more than a year of schooling in his entire life had taught himself to be a lawyer.

Abe was awkward and without the social manners of many of the other prominent citizens of Springfield, the new state capital. And yet, there was a quality about him that people came to admire. They could sense his honesty, his clear thinking. One of those who came to think highly of him was Mary Todd.

Abe was taken at once by her dark hair and pretty blue eyes. Although she had a bitter temper and a sharp tongue, Abe fell in love with her. Still he wasn't sure a marriage between them would work. It wasn't only her temper that worried him; it was also the difference in their backgrounds. She knew all the social amenities; he was socially awkward. After many arguments and even a broken engagement, the two were finally married on November 4, 1842. They would have four sons, although two would die.

In the meantime Lincoln was gaining more and more experience as a lawyer. As he traveled from court to court, Abe met a great many people. He loved to debate the issues of the day. One of the most discussed issues was slavery. Abe did not believe in slavery and yet, in those early days, he did not think the slave states should be forced to give it up. What he wanted was to stop its spread to the North and West.

As the years went by the tension between the North and the South on the issue of slavery mounted. In 1857 there came the famous case known as the Dred Scott Decision. It said that if a slave were taken by his owner into free territory, that the slave would still not be free. Lincoln spoke up against that decision. Stephen A. Douglas, who was running for the United States Senate, spoke in its defense. Lincoln was asked by his party to run against Douglas. In his speech accepting the nomination he made a statement which he believed with all his heart:

"A house divided against itself cannot stand...." He knew that one way or another the problems between the North and the South would have to be resolved.

Abe lost that election even though he received a larger share of the popular vote. Still, his campaign was not a total loss. The debates between him and Douglas gained him much recognition. He went back to his law practice and continued his travels. In his heart he knew that his political career was not over.

It was Mary who encouraged him to run for President of the United States. He never would have done it just to please his wife, but his desire to preserve the union compelled him to run. This time he won. Abraham Lincoln became the sixteenth president of the United States.

Almost immediately he found himself at war with the South. Lincoln knew that the South had many fine officers and that he did not. He had really wanted Robert E. Lee to lead the Union forces, but Lee felt his loyalty belonged to Virginia. Battles were fought and lost because Lincoln could not find the proper commander to lead his troops. He needed a general who could bring victories. Instead, he found himself surrounded by office-seekers, politicians who only wanted to feather their own nests. Lincoln worried about his country night and day.

What concerned him most was the preservation of the Union. Although he hated slavery, he still believed that it was up to the states to free their own slaves. Finally, however, he realized that the North could not win the war — that the Union could not be saved — unless he freed all the slaves. On January 1, 1863 the Emancipation Proclamation went into effect.

For the first two years of the war things went badly for the North. After the Battle of Gettysburg, however, the tide seemed to turn. It was at a ceremony held to honor the soldiers who had died during that battle that Lincoln delivered his most famous speech. Strangely enough, at the time, people failed to recognize its greatness.

"Four score and seven years ago our fathers brought forth on this continent a new nation, conceived in liberty and dedicated to the proposition that all men are created equal...."

In 1864 Lincoln gave Ulysses S. Grant command of the Union armies. Grant was a rough man — not well-liked — but he was winning battles. Before long he was considered a hero.

The Civil War, what historians call the War Between the States, came to an end on April 9, 1865. It had lasted nearly four years and had taken thousands of lives. The war had covered a battlefield so large that it had been fought from the shores of the Atlantic to the Mississippi River. It had been a dramatic war, an impossible war. Now Lincoln could thank God it was over.

Now at least he would have some time to relax. He looked forward to the evening at the theater which he and Mrs. Lincoln had planned. It would be a relief to lose himself in a play. For a little while, for an hour or two, he would forget his worries.

Still there was something troubling him. It was a dream he had had. He had dreamt that he was in a room where many people were crying. There were sounds of deep sorrow; there were men and women with tear stricken faces. In his dream he looked around and found himself in the east room of the White House. There in the center of the room was a casket. He saw himself tap the shoulder of a soldier who stood guard.

"Who is it?" he asked. "Who is dead in the White House?"

"It's the President," the soldier answered. "The President has been killed by an assassin!"

In his dream, the President just stood transfixed. He stood there for a moment or for an hour; he never knew which. When he finally woke up, it all seemed so real; so clearly could he hear the tears and the cries of those who loved him.

President Lincoln could not laugh it off. Deep inside he felt that his days were numbered. He knew that there were many who hated him. Nevertheless, he found that he was at peace with himself. He knew that what he had accomplished was done with the will of God; he knew that he had done his duty — done what he felt was best for his country.

On the night of April 14, 1865 Abraham Lincoln and his wife went to the Ford Theater to see Laura Keene star in "Our American Cousin." The show had already begun, but the beautiful Laura Keene stopped the show and began to clap her hands when the presidential party entered the box. The band started to play "Hail to the Chief." Lincoln bowed for a moment before sitting down in the upholstered rocking chair to enjoy the show. He felt secure knowing that his guard, Parker, was stationed just outside the box.

What Lincoln didn't know was that at 9:00 Parker would leave his post to get a glass of beer. Nor did he know that John Wilkes Booth, a man who hated him, was also in the theater.

John Wilkes Booth was the brother of a famous actor, Edwin Booth. John, himself an actor, could never measure up to his brother's talent. This, no doubt, bothered him. He made up his mind to do something so spectacular that he would gain national fame and put Edwin far behind. What he planned was the killing of the President.

When Booth realized that the President was unguarded, he quickly took advantage of his opportunity. This was his chance to surpass his brother Edwin. He looked through the peephole of box number seven where the President was seated. He waited until there was only one actor on stage before entering the box with his gun ready to fire. Booth put the gun against Lincoln's left ear.

The sound of laughter filled the theater. Lincoln had joined in the laughter. His last moment of conscious life was a happy one. Then, with a shot, it was all over.

Booth jumped from the ledge and landed on the stage. It was set for Act Three, Scene Two. Booth limped to his feet as Mrs. Lincoln screamed and cried for help. There were many voices crying out at once:

"It's the President!"

"The President's been shot!"

"Someone get a doctor! Hurry!"

There was such confusion that in spite of a broken leg Booth was able to hobble off the stage and even escape from Washington. He could not, however, escape the chase of an entire nation. Finally, John Wilkes Booth, the man who shot and killed President Abraham Lincoln, was trapped in a barn and shot to death.

People once again were crying in the east room of the White House. Unlike in the President's dream, however, no-one asked, "Who is dead in the White House?" Everyone knew. President Lincoln's dream had become a reality.